# Grade 5 Reading Skills:

## Reluctant Readers Edition

SPEEDY
PUBLISHING

Speedy Publishing LLC
40 E. Main St. #1156
Newark, DE 19711
www.speedypublishing.com

# Cats

Cats are small, usually furry, <u>domesticated</u>, and carnivorous mammal. They are often called housecats when kept as an indoor pet or simply cats when there is no need to <u>distinguish</u> them from other felids and felines. Cats are often valued by humans for <u>companionship</u> and their ability to hunt pests.

Cats are similar in anatomy to the other felids, with strong, flexible bodies, quick reflexes, sharp

retractable claws, and teeth adapted to killing small prey. Cats can hear sounds too faint or too high in frequency for human ears, such as those made by mice and other small animals. They can see in near darkness. Like most other mammals, cats have poorer color vision and a better sense of smell than humans.

Despite being solitary hunters, cats are a social species and cat communication includes the use of a variety of vocalizations (mewing, purring, trilling, hissing, growling and grunting), as well as cat pheromones and types of cat-specific body language.

Cats have a high breeding rate. Under controlled breeding, they can be bred and shown as registered pedigree pets, a hobby known as cat fancy. Failure to control the breeding of pet cats by neutering and the abandonment of former household pets has resulted in large numbers of feral cats worldwide, requiring population control. This has led to extinction of many bird species.

Since cats were venerated in ancient Egypt, they were commonly believed to have been domesticated there, but there may have been instances of domestication as early as the Neolithic from around 9,500 years ago (7,500 BC). A genetic study in 2007

concluded that domestic cats are _descended_ from African wildcats (Felis silvestris lybica), having diverged around 8,000 BC in West Asia.Cats are the most popular pet in the world, and are now found in almost every place where humans live.

# Reading Comprehension Exam

*A. Write all underlined words in the article.*

**B. Write at least 1 synonym for each underlined word.**

## C. Reading Comprehension Questions.

1. What are cats oftenly called?

2. Cats are similar to the anatomy of?

3. Cats have poorer _____ ?

4.   List at least 5 varieties of vocalizations of cats.

5.   In 2007, a genetic study concluded that cats are descended from?

# Dogs

The domestic dog is a domesticated <u>canid</u> which has been <u>selectively</u> bred for millennia for various behaviors, sensory capabilities, and physical attributes.

Although initially thought to have <u>originated</u> as a <u>manmade</u> variant of an extant canid species (variously supposed as being the dhole, golden jackal, or gray wolf), extensive genetic studies

undertaken during the 2010s indicate that dogs diverged from a now-extinct canid in Eurasia 40,000 years ago. Being the oldest domesticated animals, their long association with people has allowed dogs to be uniquely attuned to human behavior, as well as thrive on a starch-rich diet which would be inadequate for other canid species.

Dogs perform many roles for people, such as hunting, herding, pulling loads, protection, assisting police and military, companionship, and, more recently, aiding handicapped individuals. This impact on human society has given them the nickname "man's best friend" in the Western world. In some cultures, however, dogs are also a source of meat.

# Reading Comprehension Exam

*A. Write all underlined words in the article.*

**B. Write at least 1 synonym for each underlined word.**

## C. *Reading Comprehension Questions.*

1. How many years ago are dogs believed to extinct?

2. Domestic dogs are domestic _____.

3. Dog's are are given what nickname to humans?

4.  List at least 5 roles of dogs to human?




5.  List at least 5 breeds of dogs.

# Birds

Birds are a group of endothermic <u>vertebrates</u>, characterised by feathers, a beak with no teeth, the laying of hard-shelled eggs, a high metabolic rate, a four-chambered heart, and a <u>lightweight</u> but strong skeleton. They are from the animal class of aves. Birds have more or less <u>developed</u> wings; the only known group without wings are the moa, which is generally considered to have became extinct in the 16th century. Wings are evolved forelimbs, and most

bird species can fly. Flightless birds include ratites, penguins, and diverse <u>endemic</u> island species. Some species of birds, particularly penguins and members of the duck family, are adapted for swimming. Birds also have digestive and respiratory systems that are uniquely adapted for flight. Some birds, especially corvids and parrots, are among the most <u>intelligent</u> animals; several bird species make and use tools, and many social species pass on knowledge across generations, which is <u>considered</u> a form of culture.

Many species annually migrate great distances. Birds are social, communicating with visual signals, calls, and songs, and participating in such social behaviours as cooperative breeding and hunting, flocking, and mobbing of predators. The vast majority of bird species are socially monogamous, usually for one breeding season at a time, sometimes for years, but rarely for life. Other species have polygynous ("many females") or, rarely, polyandrous ("many males") breeding systems. Eggs are usually laid in a nest and incubated by the parents. Most birds have an extended period of parental care after hatching.

# Reading Comprehension Exam

*A. Write all underlined words in the article.*

**B. Write at least 1 synonym for each underlined word.**

## C. Reading Comprehension Questions.

1.  Scientific consensus believed that birds are advance subgroup of _____?

2.  Birds also have _____ and _____ systems that are uniquely adapted for flight

3.  Birds are of what class of animals?

4. List at least 5 kinds birds.

5. List at least 2 flightless birds.

Made in the USA
Monee, IL
29 August 2023

41802524R00021